PE

PERDITA

The Literary, Theatrical, Scandalous Life of
Mary Robinson

PAULA BYRNE

RANDOM HOUSE
New York

Published in the United States by Random House, an
imprint of The Random House Publishing Group,
a division of Random House, Inc., New York.

RANDOM HOUSE and colophon are registered trademarks of Random House, Inc.

This work was originally published in Great Britain by HarperCollins in 2004.

Longer quotations from unpublished manuscript sources are reproduced by the kind
permission of the following: Abinger Deposit, Bodleian Library, Oxford; Rear Admiral Sir
Peter and Dame Elizabeth Anson; Bristol Central Library; Folger Shakespeare Library,
Washington D.C.; Garrick Club Library; Harvard Theatre Collection; Huntington Library,
San Marino, California; Carl H. Pforzheimer Collection of Shelley and his Circle,
New York Public Library (Astor, Lenox, and Tilden Foundations); Broadley Collection,
Westminster Archives; and private collections.

LIBRARY OF CONGRESS CATALOGING-IN-PUBLICATION DATA
Byrne, Paula.
Perdita: the literary, theatrical, scandalous life of Mary Robinson/Paula Byrne.
p.   cm.
Includes bibliographical references and index.
ISBN 1-4000-6148-2
1. Robinson, Mary, 1758–1800.   2. George IV, King of Great Britain,
1762–1830—Relations with women.   3. London (England)—Social
life and customs—18th century.   4. Authors, English—18th century—
Biography.   5. Mistresses—Great Britain—Biography.
6. Actors—Great Britain—Biography.   I. Title: Literary,
theatrical, scandalous life of Mary Robinson.   II. Title.
DA538.A35B97   2005
792.02'8'092—dc22   2004051472
[B]

Random House website address: www.atrandom.com

Printed in the United States of America on acid-free paper

2 4 6 8 9 7 5 3 1

FIRST U.S. EDITION

Book design by Casey Hampton

In memory of my grandmother,
another Mary Robinson

I was delighted at the Play last Night, and was extremely moved by two scenes in it, especially as I was particularly interested in the appearance of the most beautiful Woman, that ever I beheld, who acted with such delicacy that she drew tears from my eyes.

—George, Prince of Wales

There is not a woman in England so much talked of and so little known as Mrs. Robinson.

—*Morning Herald,* April 23, 1784

I was well acquainted with the late ingenious Mary Robinson, once the beautiful Perdita . . . *the most interesting woman of her age.*

—Sir Richard Phillips, publisher

She is a woman of undoubted Genius . . . I never knew a human Being with so full a mind—bad, good, and indifferent, I grant you, but full, and over-flowing.

—Samuel Taylor Coleridge

I am allowed the power of changing my form, as suits the observation of the moment.

—Mary Robinson, writing as "The Sylphid"

ACKNOWLEDGMENTS

I gratefully acknowledge the support of the British Academy in the form of a generous research grant to help defray the cost of illustrations, permissions, microfilms, photocopies, and travel expenses.

I am very grateful to the following scholars, archivists, and librarians for assistance of various kinds: Irene Andrews, Matthew Bailey, Jennie Batchelor, Peter Beal, Jane Bradley, Siân Cooksey, Hilary Davies, Elizabeth Dunn, Julie Flanders, Amanda Foreman, Flora Fraser, Ted Gott, Katie Hickman, Alison Kenney, Jacqueline Labbe, Tom Mayberry, Judith Pascoe, Charlotte Payne, Matthew Percival, Linda Peterson, Maggie Powell, David Rhodes, Angela Rosenthal, Wendy Roworth, Diego Saglia, Helen Scott, Sharon Setzer, Stephen Tabor, Teresa Taylor, William St. Clair, Judy Simons, Jessica Vale, Steve Wharton, Frances Wilson, Robert Woof, Georgianna Ziegler.

This biography could not have been written without the resources of the following institutions: Bodleian Library, Oxford; Central Library, Bristol; Bristol Record Office; British Library (special thanks to Matthew Shaw in the Manuscripts Room and all the helpful staff in the Newspaper Division at Colindale, which was my most important source); Department of Prints and Drawings, British Museum; Cambridge University Library; Chawton House Library; Folger Shakespeare Library, Washington, D.C.; Garrick Club Library (special thanks to Marcus Risdell); Harvard Theatre Collection, Houghton Library, Harvard University (special thanks to Luke Dennis); Hertfordshire Archives and Local Studies, Hertford; Huntington Library, San Marino, California; Liverpool Record Office; the Pforzheimer

Collection at the New York Public Library (Astor, Lenox, and Tilden Foundations; special thanks to Stephen Wagner); Royal Archives and Collection (special thanks to the Registrar, Miss Pamela Clark); Shakespeare Birthplace Trust, Stratford-upon-Avon; Shakespeare Institute, Stratford-upon-Avon; Surrey Records Office; Theatre Museum, London; Wallace Collection, London; Warwick University Library; City of Westminster Archives Centre; Witt Library, London.

I am especially grateful to Rear Admiral Sir Peter and Dame Elizabeth Anson for their generosity in allowing me to see the correspondence between the Prince of Wales and Mary Hamilton and to quote from it here; also for their hospitality while I was in their home. Equal thanks are owed to the staff of the residence where the original manuscript of Mary Robinson's *Memoirs* is held and to the Trustees of the collection for permission to quote from it (special thanks to Rodney Melville). Thanks also to Rev. Nicholas Chubb for directing me to his ancestor John Chubb's portrait of Mary, to Hélène at the Tourist Office in Calais, and to Graham Dennis of Blacklock Books in Englefield Green for local knowledge when I was in search of Mary's cottage.

Thanks to my incomparable agents Andrew Wylie and Sarah Chalfant. Grateful thanks to my publishers Michael Fishwick and Kate Hyde at HarperCollins in London and Susanna Porter at Random House in New York, and Juliet Davis in the picture department at HarperCollins. Many thanks to Carol Anderson for her scrupulous copy editing.

A huge debt is owed to my friend and research assistant Héloïse Sénéchal. She has been indefatigable in her efforts and has provided assistance and companionship from the darkened rooms of the Colindale library, where we pored over eighteenth-century newspapers for days on end, to the London pubs where we shared lively discussions about Mary Robinson. Heartfelt thanks to Dr. Chris Clark for her scrupulous research on rheumatic fever. Rachel Bolger has read the entire manuscript, and I am extremely grateful for her most valuable suggestions and comments. Thanks to the mums at the Croft School, especially Tracey Rigby, Sally Manners, and Bev Clarke, who have helped in numerous ways.

Gratitude is due to my good friends who take a generous interest in my work, especially Phil and Jane Davis, Paul Edmondson, Kelvin and Faith Everest, Carol Rutter, and Stanley Wells. Thanks also to my siblings, Collette, Chris, David, Claire, Joe, and Rachael, and my wonderful parents, Tim and Clare. My children, Tom and Ellie, have shown remarkable patience, especially when I was away on research trips—thanks and love to you both. My deepest gratitude belongs to my husband and dearest friend, Jonathan Bate, who has endured the pleasures, pains, and privileges of being so long in the company of Mrs. Robinson. I salute you, and thank you for your patience and wisdom. My grandmother (also called Mary Robinson, though no relation) has been an inspiration to me all of my life. Though she died a week before the book was completed, I feel sure she would have enjoyed Mary's story. This book is for her.

CONTENTS

PART THREE: WOMAN OF LETTERS

PROLOGUE

In the middle of a summer night in 1783 a young woman set off from London along the Dover road in pursuit of her lover. She had waited for him all evening in her private box at the Opera House. When he failed to appear, she sent her footman to his favorite haunts: the notorious gaming clubs Brooks's and Weltje's; the homes of his friends, the Prince of Wales, Charles James Fox, and Lord Malden. At 2 a.m. she heard the news that he had left for the Continent to escape his debtors. In a moment of panic and desperation, she hired a post chaise and ordered it to be driven to Dover. This decision was to have the most profound consequences for the woman famous and infamous in London society as "Perdita."

In the course of the carriage ride she suffered a medical misadventure.* And she did not meet her lover at Dover: he had sailed from Southampton. Her life would never be the same again.

Born Mary Darby, she had been a teenage bride. As a young mother she was forced to live in debtors' prison. But then, under her married name of Mary Robinson, she had been taken up by David Garrick, the greatest actor of the age, and had herself become a celebrated actress at Drury Lane. Many regarded her as the most beautiful woman in England. The young Prince of Wales—who would later become Prince Regent and then King George IV—had seen her in the part of Perdita and

---

* As with many incidents in her life, the circumstances are not absolutely clear, as will be seen in chapter 15.

started sending her love letters signed "Florizel." She held the dubious honor of being the first of his many mistresses.

In an age when most women were confined to the domestic sphere, Mary was a public face. She was gazed at on the stage and she gazed back from the walls of the Royal Academy and the studios of the men who painted her, including Sir Joshua Reynolds, who was to painting what Garrick was to theater. The royal love affair also brought her image to the eighteenth-century equivalent of the television screen: the caricatures displayed in print-shop windows. Her notoriety increased when she became a prominent political campaigner. In quick succession, she was the mistress of Charles James Fox, the most charismatic politician of the age, and Colonel Banastre Tarleton, known as "Butcher" Tarleton because of his exploits in the American War of Independence. The prince, the politician, the action hero: it is no wonder that she was the embodiment of—the word was much used at the time, not least by Mary herself— "celebrity."

Her body was her greatest asset. When she came back from Paris with a new style of dress, everyone in the fashionable world wanted one like it. When she went shopping, she caused a traffic jam. What was she to do when that body was no longer admired and desired?

Fortunately, she had another asset: her voice. Whilst still a teenager, she had become a published poet. Because of her stage career, she had an intimate knowledge of Shakespeare's language—and the ability to speak it. So, as her health gradually improved, she remade herself as a professional author. Having transformed herself from actress to author, she went on to experiment with a huge range of written voices, as is apparent from the variety of pseudonyms under which she wrote: Horace Juvenal, Tabitha Bramble, Laura Maria, Sappho, Anne Frances Randall. She completed seven novels (the first of them a runaway bestseller), two political tracts, several essays, two plays, and literally hundreds of poems.[1]

Actress, entertainer, author, provoker of scandal, fashion icon, sex object, darling of the gossip columns, self-promoter: one can see why she has been described as the Madonna of the eighteenth century.[2] But celebrity has its flipside: oblivion. Mary Robinson had the unique distinction of being painted in a single season by the four great society artists of the age—Sir Joshua Reynolds, Thomas Gainsborough, John Hoppner, and George Romney—and yet within a few years of her death the Gainsborough portrait was being cataloged under the anonymous title *Portrait of a Lady with a Dog*. In the twentieth century, despite the resurgence of the art of life-writing and the enormous interest in female authors, there was not a single biography of Robinson. Before the Second World War, she was considered suitable only for fictionalized treatments, historical romances, and bodice-rippers with titles such as *The Exquisite Perdita* and *The Lost One*. In the 1950s her life was subordinated to that of the lover she thought she was pursuing to France.* A book on George IV and the women in his life did not even mention Mary's name, despite the fact that she was his first love and he remained in touch with her for the rest of her life.[3] Finally in the 1990s, feminist scholars began a serious reassessment of Robinson's literary career. However, their work was aimed at a specialized audience of scholars and students of the Romantic period in literature.[4]

When Mary Robinson began writing her autobiography, near the end of her life, there were two conflicting impulses at work. On the one hand, she needed to revisit her own youthful notoriety. She had been the most wronged woman in England, and she wanted to put on record her side of the story of her relationship with the Prince of Wales. But at the same time, she wanted to be remembered as a completely different character: the woman of letters. As she wrote, she had in her possession letters from some of the finest minds of her generation—Samuel Taylor Coleridge, William Godwin, Mary Wollstonecraft—assuring her that she was, in Coleridge's words, "a woman of genius." Royal sex scandal and the literary life do not usually cohabit between the same printed sheets, but in a biography of the woman who went from "Mrs. Robinson of Drury Lane" to "the famous Perdita" to "Mary Robinson, author," they must.

The research for this book took me from the minuscule type of the gossip columns of the *Morning Herald* in the newspaper division of the British Library at Colindale in north London to the Gothic cloister of Bristol Minster, where Mary Robinson was born. I stood below the incomparable portraits of her in the Wallace Collection tucked away off busy Oxford Street and in stately homes both vast (Waddesdon Manor)

---

* Robert Bass, *The Green Dragoon: The Lives of Banastre Tarleton and Mary Robinson* (New York, 1957)—as the title reveals, the main emphasis is on Tarleton's military career. Though Bass undertook valuable archival research, his transcriptions were riddled with errors, he misdated key incidents, and he failed to notice many fascinating newspaper reports, references in memoirs, and other sources. It is no exaggeration to say that his inaccuracies outnumber his accuracies: if Bass says that an article appeared one November in the *Morning Post*, one may rest assured that it is to be found in December in the *Morning Herald*.

and intimate (Chawton House). In the Print Room of the British Museum I pored over graphic and sometimes obscene caricatures of her; via the worldwide web I downloaded long-forgotten political pamphlets in which she figured prominently; in the New York Public Library, within earshot of the traffic on Fifth Avenue, I pieced together the letters in which Mary revealed her state of mind in the final months of her life, as she continued to write prolifically even as she struggled against illness and disability.

I found hitherto neglected letters and manuscripts scattered in the most unlikely places: in a private home in Surrey, I opened a cardboard folder and found the Prince of Wales's account of the night he saw "Perdita" at Drury Lane, written the very next day, in the first flush of his infatuation with her; in the Garrick Club, among the portraits of the great men of the theater who launched Mary's career, I discovered a letter in which she laid out her plan to rival the *Lyrical Ballads* of Wordsworth and Coleridge; and in one of the most securely guarded private houses in England—which I am prohibited from naming—I found the original manuscript of her *Memoirs*, which is subtly different from the published text. I became intimate with the perfectly proportioned face and the lively written voice of this remarkable woman. Yet as I was researching the book, people from many walks of life asked me who I was writing about: hardly any of them had heard of the eighteenth-century Mary Robinson. So I have sought to re-create her life, her world, and her work, and to explain how it was that one of her contemporaries called her "the most interesting woman of her age."[5]

Part One

ACTRESS

I

"DURING A TEMPESTUOUS NIGHT"

The very finest powers of intellect, and the proudest specimens of mental
labour, have frequently appeared in the more contracted circles of provincial
society. Bristol and Bath have each sent forth their sons and daughters of genius.
—Mary Robinson, "Present State of the Manners, Society,
etc. etc. of the Metropolis of England"

Horace Walpole described the city of Bristol as "the dirtiest great shop I ever saw." Second only to London in size, it was renowned for the industry and commercial prowess of its people. "The Bristolians," it was said, "seem to live only to get and save money."[1] The streets and marketplaces were alive with crowds, prosperous gentlemen and ladies perambulated under the lime trees on College Green outside the minster, and seagulls circled in the air. A river cut through the center, carrying the ships that made the city one of the world's leading centers of trade. Sugar was the chief import, but it was not unusual to find articles in the *Bristol Journal* announcing the arrival of slave ships en route from Africa to the New World. Sometimes slaves would be kept for domestic service: in the parish register of the church of Saint Augustine the Less one finds the baptism of a Negro named "Bristol." Over the page is another entry: Polly—a variant of Mary—daughter of Nicholas and Hester Darby, baptized July 19, 1758.[2]

Nicholas Darby was a prominent member of the Society of Merchant Venturers, based at the Merchants' Hall in King Street, an association of overseas traders that was at the heart of Bristol's commercial life. The merchant community supported a vibrant culture: a major theater, concerts, assembly rooms, coffee houses, bookshops, and publishers. Bristol's most famous literary son was born just five years before Mary. Thomas Chatterton, Wordsworth's "marvellous Boy," was the wunderkind of English poetry. His verse became a posthumous sensation in the years following his suicide (or accidental self-poisoning) at the age of 17. For Keats and Shelley, he was a hero; Mary Robinson and Samuel Taylor Coleridge both wrote odes in his memory.

Coleridge himself also developed Bristol connections. His friend and fellow poet Robert Southey, the son of a failed linen merchant, came from the city. The two young poets married the Bristolian Fricker sisters, and it was on College Green, a stone's throw from the house where Mary was born, that they hatched their "pantisocratic" plan to establish a commune on the banks of the Susquehanna River.

Mary described her place of birth at the beginning of her *Memoirs*. She conjured up a hillside in Bristol, where a monastery belonging to the order of Saint Augustine had once stood beside the minster:

> On this spot was built a private house, partly of simple and partly of modern architecture. The front faced a small garden, the gates of which opened to the Minster-Green (now called the College-Green): the west side was bounded by the Cathedral, and the back was supported by the antient cloisters of St. Augustine's monastery. A spot more calculated to inspire the soul with mournful meditation can scarcely be found amidst the monuments of antiquity.

She was born in a room that had been part of the original monastery. It was immediately over the cloisters, dark and Gothic with "casement windows that shed a dim mid-day gloom." The chamber was reached "by a narrow winding staircase, at the foot of which an iron-spiked door led to the long gloomy path of cloistered solitude." What better origin could there have been for a woman who grew up to write best-selling Gothic novels? If the *Memoirs* is to be believed, even the weather contributed to the atmosphere of foreboding on the night of her birth. "I have often heard my mother say that a more stormy hour she never remembered. The wind whistled round the dark pinnacles of the minster tower, and the rain beat in torrents against the casements of her chamber." "Through life," Mary continued, "the tempest has followed my footsteps."[3]